WALKING
IN
HEARTBEAT COUNTRY

by

J.Brian Beadle

Walking in Heartbeat Country first published in Great Britain in 2003
by Trailblazer Publishing (Scarborough)
www.trailblazerbooks.co.uk

ISBN   1 899004 45 9

Trailblazer Publishing (Scarborough)
Stoneways, South End
Burniston, Scarborough. YO13 0HP

MAPS

The maps in this book are not to scale and are for guidance only. They do not accurately portray the right of way. It is the readers responsibility not to stray from the right of way and it is strongly advised that you take the relevant Ordnance Survey map with you on the walk.

WARNING

Whilst every effort has been made for accuracy neither the publisher nor the author bear responsibility for the alteration, closure or portrayal of rights of way in this book. It is the readers responsibility not to invade private land or stray from the public right of way for walkers. All routes in the book should be treated with respect and all precautions taken before setting out. Any person using information in this book does so at their own risk.

CONTENTS

JUST A FEW WORDS

Heartbeat is the name of the popular Yorkshire Television Series filmed mainly in and around Goathland and the North York Moors. For the film series Goathland becomes the moorland village of Aidensfield,

and local establishments in Goathland have became household names - The Post Office and shop are now the Aidensfield Post Office and the Aidensfield Stores with their new names emblazoned boldly. The garage in the village is now called 'Scripp's Funeral Services' for the filming of Heartbeat and you will see some old cars and motorbikes scattered around that you might recognise. Opposite Scripp's Funeral Services is the local pub, it has two signs displayed, the Goathland Hotel on the front and The Aidensfield Arms on the side. No doubt the Hotel sign is removed during filming.

Goathland has changed from a sleepy moorland village with a handful of sightseers, walkers and hikers to a busy tourist attraction. The popularity of Goathland increased with the arrival of the magnificent steam trains of the North Yorkshire Moors Railway which stops at Goathland Station on its way from Pickering and Grosmont, then the film crews arrived to commence filming the Heartbeat series. That was several years ago and they are still filming! Now thousands of visitors each year arrive in Goathland to see the setting for themselves and if they are lucky they might arrive on a filming day and catch a glimpse of their favourite characters.

However popular Goathland has become let us not forget the local residents and businesses that have to carry on their day to day work and cope with this enormous influx of tourists. Please support them, don't become too inquisitive and let them get on with their lives. There

 are many buildings used in the filming of Heartbeat that you might spot whilst walking around the village of Goathland and the surrounding moorland. Although the wily old scoundrel Jeremiah Greengrass is no longer featured in the current series his dilapidated farmhouse is still used and is situated on a road out of Goathland. The Doctor Ferriby surgery is in the village and Goathland Railway Station has been used many times in both Heartbeat, the Harry Potter film and many others. Signposts in the village are changed when filming is in progress, the one near the War Memorial having a separate sign showing the way to Ashfordly. Another signpost you might recognise is the one opposite the car parking area at the Beckhole Junction near the Whitby road which is used frequently. You will recognise farms, waterfalls, the church and many other features not only in Goathland but as far away as Scarborough, Whitby and Ravenscar and across the moors some crosses have been featured.

I hope you enjoy walking in Heartbeat Country and I thank Yorkshire Television for allowing me to use the Heartbeat name in the title. Let us repay them, the residents and businesses and not make too much of a nuisance of ourselves whilst we enjoy the walks through this stunningly scenic part of North Yorkshire.

ROUTE 1 2½ MILES
THE ROMAN ARMY IN HEARTBEAT COUNTRY

On this walk we follow the Roman army across Wheeldale Moor as they march into 'Heartbeat' country. The Romans were masters at road building and this section across Wheeldale Moor is no exception. In fact it is one of the best preserved Roman roads in the country, although the stones are a bit haphazard now. Could the folk tale that a giant Wade and his wife Bell built the road be true? It would fit in well with many tales of a giant in the area, but I think I'll give credit to the Romans this time.

Hunt House and the road leading to it has been used by the Heartbeat team, especially the road, which has seen Greengrass's truck and Constable Nick's motorcycle many times as they go about their affairs. There is roadside parking at the start for about ten cars, please keep off the road to leave room for farm traffic to pass and do not park in the turning area.

The Facts

Distance - 2½ miles/4km

Time - 1 hour

Start - Hunt House road, grid ref. 814988

Map - OS Landranger 94 or OS Outdoor Leisure 27

Refreshment - Sandwiches and flask by the side of a gurgling beck this time

Public Toilets - None

Guide Book - Walking around the North York Moors by J.Brian Beadle has similar walks. Available from the Pickering Railway Station Shop, Low Dalby Visitor Centre, Bookshops and Tourist Information Centres

Your Route

Head off towards Hunt House in the direction of the sign showing a castle ruin. Pass a vehicular no entry sign and shortly pass Hunt House on your right. Uphill now on an unmade road and soon you reach the moor. The track then falls downhill and past a house to become narrow and grassy. Follow a sign for 'Roman Road' soon bearing right to a stile leading to the stepping stones first to cross a bog then Wheeldale Beck. This is a good place to eat your sandwiches before tackling a rather steep hill. Join the path bearing left and climbing, steeply at times, onto Wheeldale Moor but the path soon flattens out as you reach the top. Follow a wider track now which traverses the moor and reaches the Roman Road in about 150yards/metres. Turn right to follow the road. Notice the curvature and the drainage ditches of the road.

Unfortunately the top surface of the road was re-moved many years ago to be used for boundary walls and building. Keep straight ahead now fol-lowing the road to soon cross a ladder stile then continue along to a gate with a waymark and an information board. Go through the gate turning right to cross a stile. Left over the stile to join a farm road downhill. Where the farm road goes right leave it to continue straight ahead towards the beck. Go right here and over a stile. Ignore the first footbridge and continue along to the second. Cross the beck turning right to a gate. Then to an-other gate to bear right uphill along a wide track to return to your transport.

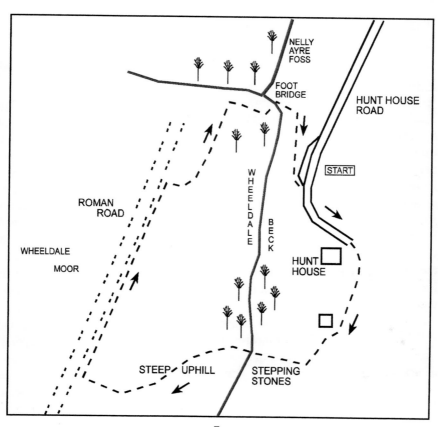

7

DARNHOLME AND BECKHOLE

D arnholme is a stunning place at anytime but in early winter the dying, golden bracken bathed in a weak yellow sun makes it something special. Beckhole is a special place also. Its stone houses huddle together in a pocket on the edge of the moor as the waters of Eller Beck gurgle past. It has a unique old Inn and a waterfall just a short walk away, the third waterfall of Goathland. See route four for two more. (*To see the waterfall, Thomason Foss, go left before the bridge and follow the beck*). Enjoy your walk through this special part of Heartbeat Country and see how many film locations you can spot along the way. There are plenty.

The Facts
Distance - 3½ miles/5½ km
Time - 2 hours
Start - Village car park Goathland, grid ref. 833013
Map - OS Landranger 94 or OS Outdoor Leisure 27
Refreshment - Beck Hole at The Birch Hall Inn, Goathland village Pub and Cafes
Public Toilets - In car park

Your Route

L eave the car park turning right, at the junction go left away from the shops. When the road sweeps right leave it to walk to the Railway Station. Cross the line to exit through the gate at the rear of the level crossing then turn immediately left. The path climbs at first parallel to the railway and beck then descends into Darnholme with superb views ahead. Bear slightly right away from the railway to a small footbridge. Keep on the obvious path towards the stepping stones - do not cross. Turn right here along a driveway at the public footpath sign. In a few yards the driveway bends to the right, turn left now to leave the drive onto a rough track. In a few yards cross the footbridge on the left to start a steep climb. There is a seat half way up, take a rest and admire the view then continue climbing to the top. Go left now over the stile at the gate and waymark. Soon pass through another gate, past a house and waymark then exit through a small gate. Take the grassy path nearest the wall now. Good views across the railway and Goathland to the moors. When the path splits keep on the right path nearest the wall. Soon you come to a waymark post. Go left here as directed onto a narrow path through the bracken, keep a sharp eye out in a few yards taking an even narrower path through the bracken on the left. The path falls and soon reaches another waymark post at a crossroad of tracks. Turn left here and descend through the bracken. Shortly cross a wide grassy path then keep descending through the bracken. Care now, this one is very steep and can be slippery. Bear right at the wall then keep right away from the bridge. Do not cross the footbridge over the river! Follow the fence round to the right then take care on a narrow path with a precipitous drop when climbing back onto the moor. Follow the wall in front of you passing a farm then join a farm track. Follow this almost to the next farm then turn left towards the signpost opposite. Turn right at the sign to exit along the farm drive. Go left at the road over the railway bridge then down a steep hill into Beckhole. Stop at the Birch Hall Inn for a pint and a 'Beck Hole Butty'. Leave the Inn, cross the road and enter the large gate to walk along to another gate. Turn left past Incline Cottage then pass through a gate to climb the old railway incline. At the top turn right through the gate and follow the road back to Goathland.

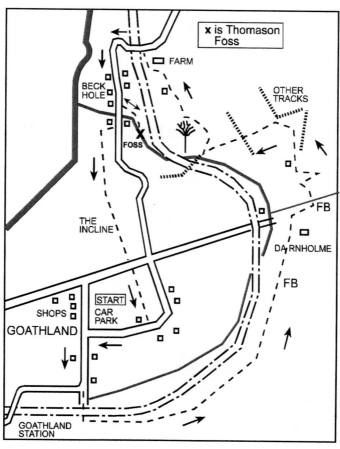

DISASTER ON THE INCLINE

On this walk you use the railway incline where carriages were hauled up and down on a rope. It was powered by water which was used as ballast . Almost a mile in length it has had its share of accidents, probably the most serious being on a frosty evening on the 13th of February 1864. The engine was disconnected and the carriages attached to a

INCLINE COTTAGE

brake van which itself was attached to a rope. The carriages were then pushed over the incline in a controlled descent. On this fateful February day when only a few hundred yards down the incline the rope snapped and the carriages hurtled down the incline picking up terrific speed. The line curves to the right at the bottom to cross the beck. This was too much for the speeding carriages. They derailed killing two passengers and injuring fourteen others. Today you can walk the incline, but listen carefully and you might just hear the screams of the ghosts of the terrified passengers as they hurtle down the incline to their deaths!

The Facts

Distance - 4 miles/6.4km

Time - 2 hours

Start - Goathland village car park, grid ref. 833013

Map - OS Landranger 94 or OS Outdoor Leisure 27

Refreshment - Along the way have a Beckhole Butty at the Birch Hall Inn at Beckhole or call in at the Aidensfield Arms at the finish of the walk

Public Toilets - In the car park

Guide Book - Walking around Ryedale, Pickering & Helmsley by J.Brian Beadle has similar walks. Available from the Pickering Railway Station Shop, Low Dalby Visitor Centre, Bookshops and Tourist Information Centres

Your Route

Leave the car park past the toilets then go left into a field at the sign for 'Grosmont Rail Trail'. You are now on the track of the old railway at the top of the incline. Continue downhill to the road. Cross the road and keep straight ahead down the old railway incline. After a pleasant walk pass through a gate into the grounds of Incline Cottage. Pass the cottage then go left at the sign 'To The Mallyan'. Shortly the path climbs steeply, at the top there are good views behind you. Pass through a couple of gates and a field before descending down to the Beck. Soon you see a signpost, go left here uphill in the direction of Goathland. It is a long stiff climb but eventually you reach the Mallyan Hotel at the top. Go left onto the road now passing or dropping in at the Prudom House Tea Rooms. Opposite the tea rooms turn right at the footpath sign for 'Abbots House'. Just past 'The Beacon' guest house go straight ahead through a gate into a field. Keep straight ahead at the next gate/stile and shortly another stile. Soon the path goes right over a footbridge and stone stile then in a few yards goes left over a stile into a caravan park. Bear right through the caravan park to eventually reach the old railway track. Go left here along the old railway track. At the end of the track you reach Goathland. Opposite you is Scripp's Garage and on the right the Aidensfield Arms. After taking a look at the garage and having a bite to eat in the pub walk towards the shops, keeping the garage on your right and in a few yards go right back to the car park.

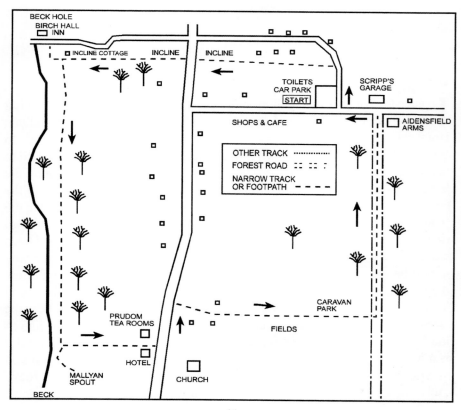

ROUTE 4   6 MILES
TWO WATERFALLS TO MAKE THE HEARTBEAT

Nelly Aire Foss, Mallyan Spout and Thomason Foss are the three water falls of Heartbeat Country. Two are accessed on this walk from the western side of Goathland, the third is near Beck Hole and is mentioned in route two. Let us start with the walk to the Mallyan Spout and Nelly Aire Foss. Nelly Aire Foss uses the water of West Beck for its fall whereas the Mallyan Spout uses the water of a tributary and falls into West Beck. Both are completely different and can be quite tricky to get to so go well prepared with good footwear as there are slippery rocks and a gully to negotiate.

The Facts

Distance - 6 miles/9.6km

Time - 3 hours

Start - Goathland village car park grid ref. 833013

Map - OS Landranger 94 or OS Outdoor Leisure 27

Refreshment - The Mallyan Hotel and Prudom house Tea Rooms, both near the start

Public Toilets - In the Goathland village car park

Your Route

Leave the car park and walk past the village shops. At the junction go left then in ¾ of a mile turn right on the footpath at the side of the Mallyan Hotel through an iron gate signed to the Mallyan Spout. The path leads to West Beck and is steep and sometimes slippery. At the beck turn left signed to the Mallyan Spout. It isn't far but be careful it is quite tricky negotiating the large slippery rocks as you pass the waterfall. Continue along the bank of the beck all the way to the bridge where you must leave the beck and exit onto the road. Turn left and climb a very steep hill. At the second sharp left bend go right at the footpath sign to a gate. Pass through the gate past a house and keep close to the wall on your right. Follow the path near the wall for some way until it becomes a fence and in a few yards (metres) turns sharp right. Follow the fence and the sign directing you to the Foss. At the end of the fence you have a choice. Go left for an easy route down to the beck but you will be at the wrong side of the Foss. If you turn right and walk carefully along the line of the fence, you will see the Foss at the bottom of the gully. Please be careful it is a narrow path on top of a precipitous edge. I do not recommend that you attempt to descend to the bottom of the gully as it is a tricky, slippery rocky gully which is difficult and dangerous. You are in mountain goat territory!

When you have seen everything return back to the sign at the corner. Go diagonally right now on a path leading up to Hunt House Road. Turn right onto the road and walk along to Hunt House in the dip and go left at the bridleway sign to climb up onto the moor. If you lose the path head 50 yards (metres) to the right of a small tree at the top and follow a gully to the summit. You will see a large cairn ahead of you, ignore this and turn left onto a narrow path which follows the edge of the hill and passes many cairns along the way. If you see any paths leading off ignore them and eventually you will arrive at a Tarn. Go right past the tarn then left and over the hill to the road. Right here then left past the church and the Mallyan Hotel. Continue on into Goathland and the car park.

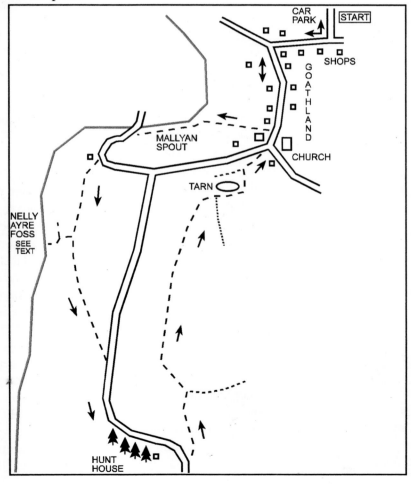

ROUTE 5   7½ MILES
WHERE THE MOORS MEET THE SEA

Heartbeat leaves its Goathland location at times to film at Scarborough, Whitby and other sites along the Heritage coast. This walk takes us midway between the two to onto high moors, tall cliffs and splendid views. Starting from Ravenscar with the Raven Hall Hotel situated on the site of a Roman Signal Station on the highest part of these tremendous cliffs we walk onto the moors to soak up views into Cleveland in the north and Flamborough Head to the south and towards Goathland in the west. On the coast the cliffs sweep round to Robin Hoods Bay and out to Ness Point. Take your camera with you for this is a landscape opportunity not to be missed, a true gem of beauty on the North Yorkshire coast.

The Facts
Distance - 7½ miles (12.3km)
Time - 3 hours
Start/Parking - Roadside at Ravenscar grid ref. 980015
Map - OS Landranger 94 or OS Outdoor Leisure 27
Refreshment - Foxcliffe Tea Rooms Ravenscar just down the road
Public Toilets - Ravenscar near the roadside park

Your Route

Park along the road leading to the Raven Hall Hotel. Walk uphill with your back to the hotel, past the telephone box and church until you arrive at a road junction and bridleway sign going right. Turn along this road which is called Robin Hood Road formerly School Lane. When the surfaced road finishes keep straight ahead onto a wide track which soon narrows as it starts to climb onto the moor. The path splits shortly, follow the bridleway straight ahead to the left of Brickyard Cottage. The track climbs still to a stone parapet then shortly there is a choice of route. Take the one climbing left to the holly bush. This will take you to the road. Turn left at the road up a steep hill to the radio tower. Turn right at the sign 'Bridleway' onto a wide track across the moor. The view is fantastic from here, a 360 degree vista! Watch your step as you approach a bog and keep straight ahead when the track splits. Soon you reach a junction of tracks, turn right here as directed by the blue waymark. As you cross the moor you will see a large stone on the left. It is inscribed 'H Dal', an arrow and 1902. I can only assume it is a waymark stone pointing to Harwood Dale several miles away. Continue straight on past the stone to the farm. At the entrance to 'The Ranch' there is a signpost with four routes marked. Take

14

the bridleway signed to Robin Hoods bay through the farmyard. Exit the farmyard through a small gate at the rear onto a bridleway to a gate. Through the gate walk across the field diagonally left following the farmers tracks to go downhill to the wood at the bottom of the field through a gate to a junction of tracks and a signpost. Go right now signed to Spring Hill. At Spring Hill Farm continue straight through the farmyard and downhill on a loose surfaced track. Cross the bridge then climb up to soon meet the road at the farm. Turn right onto the road then in almost a mile cross the old railway bridge to some houses. Look carefully for the signed bridleway on the right opposite the White Lodge. Downhill to a footbridge now then straight ahead uphill across the field to a gate. Bear left now along a hedged bridleway turning right at the top then left to climb up to the old railway track. At the track turn left to return to Ravenscar in about three miles with fantastic coastal views all the way.

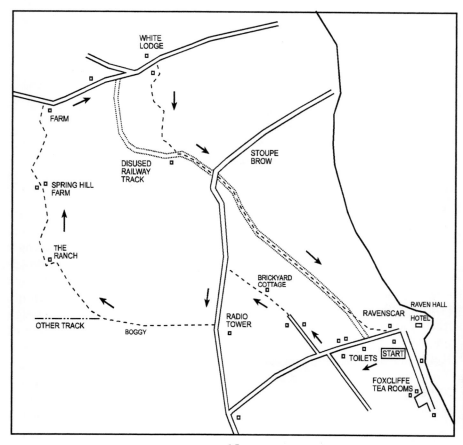

ROUTE 6
8½ MILES

THREE CROSSES ON GOATHLAND MOOR

The parking area and sign post to Beckhole is seen often in Heartbeat with PC Nick riding past it on his motorcycle. The views across Eskdale and Goathland are superb from this point. As you walk across the moor just think back to medieval times when these tracks, crosses and guide stones were along the main roads that traversed the moors. Pack horses and their attendants walked miles transporting salt, fish and many other goods to and from the coast. This was legitimate trade, unlike other goings on carrying goods from the coast which was probably a product of France! Yes, smuggling was big business in these parts for many years.

The Facts
Distance - 8½ miles/13½km

Time - 3 hours

Start - Driving from Whitby turn off the A169 at the Goathland sign. The parking area is on the left opposite the Beckhole junction, grid ref. 852028

Map - OS Landranger 94

Refreshment - None

Public Toilets - Take to the woods!

Guide Book - Walking the Ridges & Riggs of the North York Moors by J.Brian Beadle has similar walks. Available from the Pickering Railway Station Shop, Low Dalby Visitor Centre, Bookshops and Tourist Information Centres

Your Route

Walk away from the road onto a wide track near the National Park board. Pass through a gate then cross the A169 with care to another gate and stile onto the moor. Along a wide stony track now soon passing a couple of marker stones and a signpost. Keep straight ahead here going downhill past the rusty pylons and a confirmation bridleway sign. Soon go through a large gate/stile as you walk nearer to the trees. Shortly you start to climb, bearing right now away from the trees. Climbing higher now on this rough track good views across to the coast appear on the left. At the junction of tracks and waymarks bear right still climbing and soon meet another track. Keep straight ahead until you reach a gate. Do not go through the gate but bear left to follow the line of the fence on your right. In the distance you will see Anne's Cross. Soon you walk past the cross and head on towards Lilla. Eventually you reach the top of the hill. Bear right here through a small gate then in a few yards (metres) go left past a marker post. Not far to a signpost where you must go right now signed to Saltergate, then shortly take a narrow path left through the heather to arrive at Lilla Cross which stands proud in splendid isolation. This is a good place to eat your sandwiches as you soak up the all round view from coast to moor. When you can pull yourself away retrace your steps to the small gate, this time keeping straight ahead towards the forest.

Follow the undulating forest road for one and a half miles until you join another road. Bear left here, then in about a quarter of a mile go left into a wide clearing which you will clearly see leads onto the moor. Not far out of the forest you climb gently to reach York Cross. Continue climbing for a while then descend gently on a rough track. You might recognise it as the track you came on. Continue along to a gate/stile then climb past the pylons to the road. Cross the road to return to the parking area.

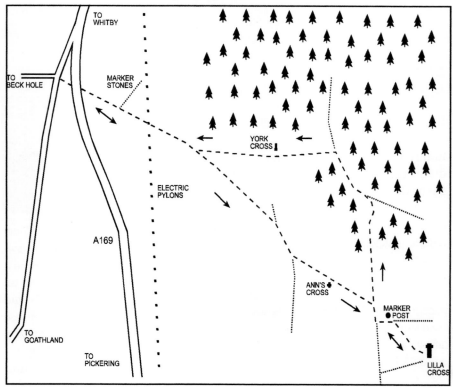

ROUTE 7   6½MILES
THE TRAVERSE OF TWO HOWES RIGG

There are more than 2000 Howes on the North York Moors standing as landmarks on the high ground. Bronze Age man buried important people with their personal belongings in these Howes. On excavation of their remains daggers, clothing and even canoes have been found in these ancient graves, although many of the howes were robbed and the treasures stolen. Maybe in the next millennium Heartbeat memorabilia might be found around Goathland with Scripp's Garage contents becoming collectors items!

The Facts

Distance - 6½ miles/10½km
Time - 3 hours
Start - Village car park Goathland, grid ref. 833013
Map - OS Landranger 94 or OS Outdoor Leisure 27
Refreshment - Goathland village Pub and Cafes
Public Toilets - In car park
Guide Book - Walking the Ridges & Riggs of the North York Moors by J.Brian Beadle has similar walks. Available from the Pickering Railway Station Shop, Low Dalby Visitor Centre, Bookshops and Tourist Information Centres

Your Route

Start from the village car park and head off through the village past the shops. Bear left at the signpost and walk along to the church. Almost opposite the church turn right along the Egton road. In a hundred yards or so turn left onto the grass at the bridleway sign. Keep on the path as it climbs away from the road. Look onto the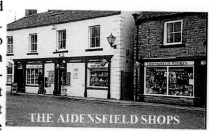

THE AIDENSFIELD SHOPS

horizon on your left and when you see a seat go left and in a few yards meet another track which takes you uphill and past the seat. *(If you arrive at signpost you have missed the seat!)* Continue across the grassy track to arrive at a tarn. Bear right now alongside the tarn. Where the path splits take the one on the right nearest the tarn. Follow this path for some time climbing gently and passing several cairns to guide you. If you look to the right onto Hunt House road you might see the Heartbeat team at work. Eventually you reach the top and a large cairn. Keep straight on to the next cairn then continue along towards a large cairn on the left on the moor. Before you reach this cairn turn right to descend off the moor towards Hunt House. The path disappears at times but keep heading towards Hunt House at the left side of the fir trees in front of you. When you meet the road/track go left to climb for a short way. Downhill soon and past a house. Soon the path goes right to a stile. Do not take this path but turn left over a rickety wooden footbridge to climb onto the moor. The path is quite steep at times but persevere and you soon reach the top. Straight ahead now to Simon Howe which is the highest point in front of you on the horizon. At the howe stop and admire the grand views all around then go left onto a path through the heather towards the two howes in the distance. At the marker post take the path on the right and eventually you reach the howes. Continue along keeping the howes on your right joining a path downhill to soon reach the tarn which you passed soon after the start. Go right past the tarn to return on the path past the seat which you came on then follow the road back to Goathland.

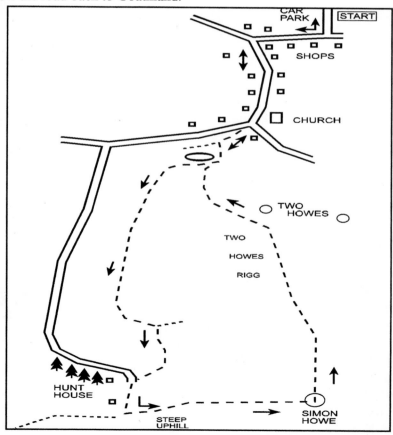

ROUTE 8

ALONG STEPHENSON'S RAILWAY TRACK

S omething different this time, why not catch the steam train to Grosmont and use this walk to return to Goathland? This scenic route uses the old railway track which was opened in 1836 by George Stephenson as a horse drawn tramway. After many successful years the line was bought by "Mr. Railway" himself, George Hudson in 1845. He converted the line to carry steam engines and used this track until 1865.

The Facts

Distance - 5 miles/8km
Time - 2 hours
Start - Grosmont Station, grid ref.. 828053
Map - OS Landranger 94 or OS Outdoor Leisure 27
Refreshment - Along the way have a Beckhole Butty at the Birch Hall Inn at Beckhole or pop into the Signals Buffet on the platform at Grosmont, try the home made pasties they are delicious
Public Toilets - On the platform or in the village

Your Route

L eave the platform turning left over the level crossing. Immediately over the crossing take the path on the right signed to 'Loco shed and Goathland'. Cross the bridge over the Murk Esk then turn left uphill past the school and church signed as 'Rail Trail'. Exit through a gate turning right along the 'Rail Trail'. Uphill through a gate then left through another gate at the sign for 'Goathland, Rail Trail'. Downhill now past the engine sheds and workshop on the left through a couple of gates to turn right onto Stephenson's old railway track. In about a mile cross a road and keep straight ahead at the houses and go through the gate

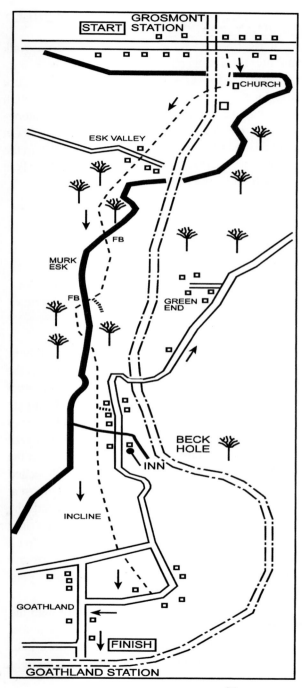

to rejoin the track. Soon you will see a small plaque with details about the old railway. Keep straight ahead passing the odd bridge and field or two to enter the woods soon bearing right over another bridge over the river, ignoring the steps on the left! Pass through a small gate and at the sign keep straight ahead signed to 'Goathland Rail Trail'. Shortly you will see the houses of Beck Hole coming into view on the left. The path splits here, if you are in need of refreshment at the Birch Hall Inn bear left, cross the stile and walk to the village. If not continue straight ahead and follow the path over the beck and past Incline Cottage to climb the incline. At the top of the incline exit through a gate onto the road. Go right here then at the memorial go left to return to the car park or if you came by train continue past the car park to the Railway Station.

21

MAY BECK & JOHN BOND'S SHEEPHOUSE

Many of the scenes filmed in Heartbeat are remote from Goathland, this walk takes in several potential sites for filming all with there own unique character of the North York Moors. Of all the forests in the North Riding Forest Park Sneaton must have the best features. A Hermitage, an old sheephouse, a high waterfall, a ghostly old cottage, gurgling becks, and a pleasant picnic area alongside a dark moorland stream all surrounded by beautiful heather moorland. On this walk we visit the ruin of John Bond's Sheephouse in a sheltered valley in the forest. On the way there are grand views across the moors to the sea. The walk is only short but perhaps long enough for a cold winter's day.

The Facts
Distance - 4 miles/6.4km
Time - 2 hours
Start - Maybeck Picnic area, grid ref. 892024
Map - OS Outdoor Leisure 27
Refreshments - May Beck, ice cream, crisps hot & cold drinks in summer

Your Route

Leave the car park at May Beck and walk up the road you came on. In 100yds/mtrs at a large stone turn right at the footpath sign. It is quite a pull up the hillside through the bracken but the path is well worn. Soon you meet a rather awkward stile, clamber over it and continue climbing on the well trodden path which opens out to give grand views across May Beck to the forest. At the top of the climb exit over a stile into a field and walk straight ahead near to the stone wall on your left to pass by a ruined building to another stile. Bear slightly left over the stile to soon join a wide track bearing right and climbing to a gate silhouetted against the sky at the top of the hill. Exit onto the moor and walk to a signpost at a crossroad of paths. Turn right onto a wide path which falls gently towards the forest. There are good views towards the coast from here. At the fork keep right then at the fence cross the stile into the forest. Bear left now onto a forest path keeping the fence on your left. The path soon bends to the right, descends and crosses a footbridge to John Bond's Sheephouse. This is a good place to eat your sandwiches!

Opposite the ruined sheephouse go left at the footpath sign and climb into the forest through a canopy of fir trees onto a golden carpet of needles. Keep almost straight ahead now to stay on the most obvious path through the forest until eventually you meet a wide forest road. Go left here, then in a few yards go right then left onto a parallel forest path. Continue along to soon meet another forest road. Right now and downhill for a short way until you see a wide path on your right going into the forest with a confirming footpath sign. Walk downhill though the trees for some time, alongside babbling becks until you meet a small gate. Continue through the gate then just before the footbridge at the bottom of the hill go right uphill through a small gate to climb quite steeply into the forest. As the path opens out watch out for a boggy section! Keep well clear. Follow the obvious track as it becomes a narrow path again, twisting and turning as it climbs through the trees. At last the path descends to a footbridge. Go left over the bridge and follow the undulating path through the bracken. You will hear a waterfall beneath you but might have difficulty seeing it. The path passes a seat, take a rest if you need one and admire the view, then continue your way on the footpath which eventually descends to May Beck and the car park.

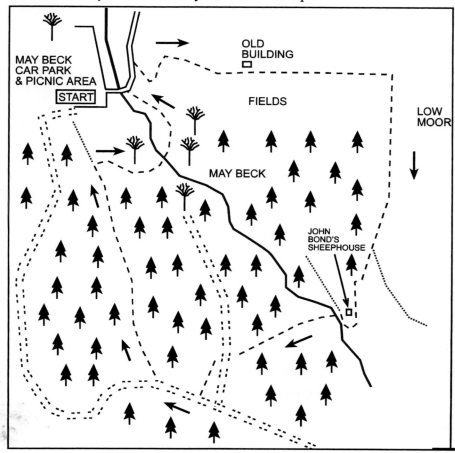

TRAILBLAZER BOOKS

CYCLING BOOKS
Mountain Biking around the Yorkshire Dales
Mountain Biking the Easy Way
Mountain Biking in North Yorkshire
Mountain Biking on the Yorkshire Wolds
Mountain Biking for Pleasure
Mountain Biking in the Lake District
Mountain Biking around Ryedale, Wydale & the North York Moors
Exploring Ryedale, Moor & Wold by Bicycle
Beadle's Bash - 100 mile challenge route for Mountain Bikers

WALKING BOOKS
Walking into History on the Dinosaur Coast
Walking around the Howardian Hills
Walking in Heartbeat Country
Walking the Riggs & Ridges of the North York Moors
Short Walks around the Yorkshire Coast
Walking on the Yorkshire Coast
Walking to Abbeys, Castles & Churches
Walking around the North York Moors
Walking around Scarborough, Whitby & Filey
Walking to Crosses on the North York Moors
Walks from the Harbour
Walking in Dalby, the Great Yorkshire Forest
Walking in the Footsteps Captain Cook
Ten Scenic Walks around Rosedale, Farndale & Hutton le Hole
Twelve Scenic Walks from the North Yorkshire Moors Railway
Twelve Scenic Walks around the Yorkshire Dales
Twelve Scenic Walks around Ryedale, Pickering & Helmsley

DOING IT YOURSELF SERIES
Make & Publish Your Own Books

THE EXPLORER SERIES
Exploring Ryedale, Moor & Wold by Bicycle

YORKSHIRE BOOKS
Curious Goings on in Yorkshire
The Trailblazer Guide to Crosses & Stones on the North York Moors

For more information please visit our web site:
www.trailblazerbooks.co.uk